Mindset for Success

*Shut Up Your Inner Critic and
Get the Life You Want*

Jack M. Allen, Ph.D.

Jack M. Allen, Ph.D.

ISBN: 1985582929
ISBN-13: 978-1985582927

DEDICATION

Dedicated to the love of my life for putting up with me
all these years as I wrestled with this stuff.
You are a patient trainer of
old dogs.

Jack M. Allen, Ph.D.

.

CONTENTS

ACKNOWLEDGMENTS

Thank you to over four hundred clients who once believed they weren't good enough, didn't have enough, or felt unseen forces holding them back. No longer hindered, you're creating the life of your dreams. You patiently proved these concepts, and I'm grateful.

Thank you, Beth, for design, and Miranda, for distribution. Thank you, Amanda, Ann, Tim, Val, Mike for generous assistance. Mom, thank you too--we may not have started off all that great together, but we sure are ending well!

Janet, *you are my sunshine.* Thank you most of all for encouraging me, proofing endless pages, and offering feedback in spite of stubbornness.

May our tribe increase.

Jack M. Allen, Ph.D.

INTRODUCTION

Congratulations for committing to take your life to the next level. Everyone in our "tribe" has a personal desire for the good life. We believe there's more to life than what we've experienced so far, and we want to find it, secure it, and share it with our loved ones.

I've found that when humans consistently grow and expand boundaries, we feel most alive. Our brains are perfectly designed to achieve whatever we believe we can achieve. God has given us the desires of our hearts, and the tools to go get them. Now is the day to learn to use those tools and begin enjoying your life more than ever before. Perhaps you agree that we want to achieve and to spend time in a joyful, creative state of mind, but it just doesn't last, does it?

If you're like most of us, you've had a great idea. You just knew that idea was your ticket. You imagined providing a nicer life for your family. Your own home, paid off cars, better schools, relaxing vacations--imagine it now and it feels good, doesn't it?

As you stepped toward achieving your idea, your brain seesawed between relaxed confidence and stressed out misery. An inner critic started bugging you with nagging doubts. You aren't good enough. You don't have what it takes. No one in your family amounted to much. You can't afford it. You don't have time. Life is passing you by. You're not far enough along.

Get ready to shut that critic up. Successful people have learned to control it. You will too.

~~~~~~

Success in life is the sum of the mindset we create,
the action we take,
and time.

~~~~~~

You'll learn time-tested, scientifically proven concepts and tactics that increase your ability to set better goals and see them through. If you stay with it, you'll achieve the life you want.

You'll benefit from 40 years of study in motivation, psychology, ethics, and neuroscience. Over 75,000 hours of my head buried in countless books, articles, research studies, and interviews have gone into creating this material. It was tested for over four years on hundreds of people to find the formula that helps our brains work as they were designed, and to give you the life of your dreams.

For thousands of years, the world's greatest thinkers speculated on how to have "the good life." After all that time, the research concludes something you probably already know: mindset matters most! This program helps you develop the same mindset that propels the world's most successful people to have the good life.

Here's the key: commitment. People living their best life commit to do what it takes. They *take personal responsibility for everything in their life, and they learn from every failure.* They get help and give credit to people who help them. To get what you want out of this program means personal responsibility to do the work in ten areas that make an impact across your life:

- Balancing the Areas of Your Life
- Adopting a Positive Attitude
- Gaining Confidence

- Creating a Clear Vision for Your Life
- Setting Goals
- Time Management
- Energy Management
- Stress Management
- Money Management
- Relationship Management

You will receive proven tips to create your best life. Commit now to doing the work. If you do, you will look up one day and realize that you have the life you dream of.

That's a fact,
Jack

Bonus: Watch the video introduction at vimeo.com/253071921

Jack M. Allen, Ph.D.

1

NOT BALANCING MEANS FALLING ON YOUR BUTT

Watch the chapter 1 video at vimeo.com/253082699

We hear a lot about life balance, but having a balanced life is a myth. Life is far too complex to balance. There are five parts to a great life, and each one needs different amounts of attention at different times. Having the best life means constantly balancing each of these areas.

In this chapter, you will learn:

- The five areas of life.
- Where you stand in each area.
- Which area you want to work on next.

The Five Areas of Life

Living the good life means taking right actions in every area of life. Too many people have focused too long on heating up one area while the others grew cold. I find that the most common mistake Americans make is to focus on their career to the neglect of building wealth, relationships, health, and spirituality. People buy into a lie believing that a satisfying career alone makes life meaningful. A career is important, but hardly the most important thing in life. By the same token, the one who focuses solely on any single area--even family, which is the great idol of our day--finds regret as the other areas grow cold.

Our first exercise identifies and measures your level of satisfaction in each of the five areas of life. Please note that I ask for *your* level of satisfaction. I'm not interested in what society thinks you should say, or the answer that pleases your mother. To become successful requires that you think for yourself.

You may notice an absence of categories like romance or intellectual learning. My research finds that the five we measure (health, wealth, career, spirituality, and relationships) offer plenty of information to get most people started. Getting started is often half the battle!

Some people want us to think of the five areas as plates spinning on the top of sticks, like we saw in the old circus act. The performer watches for a wobbly plate and hits it just right to keep it spinning. He hops back and forth, trying to keep the plates spinning and we watch for a plate to fall and smash on the ground. This is a terrible analogy for our lives. It assumes we can balance everything, and that not doing so means brokenness and losing. But that's not true.

Many times, an area of life must be neglected for months to avoid a crisis in another area. If your child is sick--really sick--you may need to neglect your career to save her life. That's an excellent trade, and your career will spring back to life when you return to it.

Think of the five areas as pots of different soups sitting on a stove. Ideally, you keep them all bubbling hot on five burners because it takes all five to have the nourishment you need. But, because the human mind can only focus on one thing at a time, it's like you have only one burner. So, you move the pots to the flame to heat them up as needed. Start heating up whichever pot of soup you need. It's that simple.

You will soon realize that these areas are not independent, but highly dependent on one another. Such is the beauty of a mindset bent toward progress. Your goal is to identify areas in need of heat and make progress heating them up. Each is important, none is neglected.

We'll look at each area to get the big picture. Then you can decide how to score them in your life. As we attend to each area of life in its turn, the others tend to grow a bit as though a tide were coming in and lifting all the boats.

~~~~~~

Life balance is a myth. Life balancing is a fact, Jack.
~~~~~~

Health

As people age, we often hear them say something like, "When you have your health, you have everything." This is utter nonsense, for health without the other four is poverty, loneliness, and misery at its worst.

That said, health is often the easiest one to improve (and the most neglected), and without paying attention to it, most people handcuff all the other areas. A fool neglects health.

Health includes two dimensions: physical and mental. Attaining physical health is almost always as simple as eating right and exercising. Eat junk and sit all day and you can guarantee less physical health. Move more and eat better, and you'll see that health improves. You are intelligent enough to know that, and so is every American.

Why then are most people so fat? Why do we suffer from so many avoidable physical problems? Because our mental health lives in a broken down shack of laziness, entitlement, and false beliefs. Most of these are avoidable. (More on this in chapter three.)

One of the greatest discoveries of humanity is that in the brain a belief leads immediately to action. If someone believes a lie, their brain dumps chemicals into their bloodstream that causes their body to take immediate action in the wrong direction.

First, get your mind right, and then take action to get your body tight. Most people believe exercise is too hard and they take action in that direction. They sit around lazily and their bodies grow. And grow. And grow.

I can hear the howling at that last line. Someone wants to argue about a hypothetical person with a physical impairment or disability that prevents them from exercising. Ask any physical therapist and you'll hear a trained professional say that most people are healthy enough to exercise and almost everyone is lazy. A physical disability is not your problem. Start sweating.

As for the mental limitations we place on ourselves, well those are easier to defeat than a lazy butt. There is not time in this brief chapter to teach you all you need to know to defeat self-defeating thoughts, but you can definitely get a start and help yourself. After 750 clients, I can assure you that most people defeat themselves by listening to the lies of their inner critic, and those noisy lies are the most powerful barrier to their success.

I find three categories of mental lies:

- Comparison lies
- Scarcity lies
- Bogeyman lies

Comparisons are common. People tell themselves they're not good enough, not pretty enough, not smart enough, not far along enough, or just plain not enough. We often compare ourselves to others, and it's dumb. You are unique. You run your own race. No one else has your mix of talent and experience, or lives within your circumstances.

Comparisons are silly and useless, the stuff of high school drama. Successful people do not compare themselves to their parents, siblings, friends, or--and this really is the dumbest thing in the world--to celebrities. None of those people are you, and the celebrity group are the most screwed up, narcissistic, attention-cravers of all. Be nice to others, but do not compare yourself to them!

Scarcity lies are my least favorite and also embarrassingly stupid. People tell themselves they cannot afford it (it being the thing that will make life much better) while spending money on expensive cell phone and cable television plans, electronic and kitchen gadgets, and credit card debt. You have all the money you need right now to take a step toward the good life unless you waste it on junk. And even then, you probably have enough to get started.

I've found that as soon as most people start doing what it takes to afford the things that make their life better, money flows toward them. Not mumbo jumbo magic, but clearing away brain cluttering barriers so that they can see creative ways to make and save money. They've trained their mind to see the right things.

Another person tells herself she does not have time. No time for what? For the thing that will give her a better life. She has time to watch idiotic television dramas, but not to read something that will make her more valuable at work. The fact is that you and I have just as much time as the wealthiest person on the planet--168 hours per week--but successful people invest time in things that matter while most people waste time on things that do not matter. You have time, invest it wisely.

Bogeyman lies are those that imagine an unseen force bent toward their destruction. I once thought God was punishing me, then I read enough to realize he was not, but I was punishing myself by creating a stupid lie. People think luck is against them; an unseen force keeping them down. They believe an unknown enemy is against their success. These are all fabrications.

If you believe in God, focus on the good things provided for your enjoyment. If you believe in any spiritual force, notice the benefits you enjoy from unseen and unexplainable miracles all around you.

~~~~~~

Stop lying to yourself! You are good enough, and you have all the time and money you need to move toward a better life.

~~~~~~

Train your brain to notice more blessings by being grateful for what you have now. You will be surprised that after a couple weeks, your mental state will improve. You'll start realizing that God is for you, and your enemies are too busy being idiots to worry about you!

Wealth

Add up all your assets (house, car, clothes, cash, furniture, all of it). Subtract all your debts (mortgage, student loans, credit card balances, anything else you owe). The result is your financial net worth.

Despite what most advertisers want you to believe, your financial worth has nothing to do with your worth as a person. Do not confuse the two--doing so is a comparison lie that capsizes mental health.

Do pay attention to how you invest your money. A new car goes down in value faster than a used car. A real estate investment tends to appreciate more than a stock market investment, and way more than furniture, clothes, or cars.

~~~~~~

The single fastest way to build wealth in the USA
is to own your own business.

~~~~~~

To learn more about building wealth, read and ask for advice from people who have done what you want to do. If you have less than $100,000 net worth, do not ask the millionaire who started with half a million. Ask for help from someone who started where you're starting.

When I started, I had to come up with $10 or my landlord promised he would throw my stuff in the street. Now that I think about it, I had a stereo worth about $20, a suit worth half that, and not much else. I was $10 away from homeless, though I did not feel impoverished at the time. I felt like I needed to make some changes. I guess the changes worked since my wife and I realized we had enough to retire at 55.

Career

Think of your career as solving other people's problems. People get paid to solve problems and not much else. Sadly, most Americans hate their jobs, and stay in jobs that make them crazy and keep them broke. I've found that very few people go to work trying to solve someone else's problem. Maybe that's the problem.

Many people believe work is very hard. They heard their parents complaining about sore feet, meaningless tasks, and horrible bosses. Those words stuck in their young minds and became beliefs that work is hard and meaningless. Your parent's crappy job (or lousy attitude about their job) doesn't influence yours anymore than you let it.

If your parents had a rotten career, that's their fault, not yours.

You will spend about ten hours per day working or thinking about work. Find something you like and that you do well enough to get paid for it. Then improve until you can do that thing exceptionally well. You'll be surprised how being the best at anything will add meaning to your life and fatten up your bank account.

Spirituality

You want to know the most powerful category? This one. Sound spirituality builds confidence in your ability to solve any problem. Fuzzy spirituality tries to cover all possibilities by naming its benefactor after an impersonal force like "the universe." But an impersonal force can no more give you personalized direction than a light bulb can (sure, it may offer some light, even warmth, but not personalized direction).

I think one reason people are wandering toward an impersonal spirituality is because so many people who claim a personal God are mean as hell. We all see people who say that they believe in God's kindness and grace while they act hatefully toward others, which makes no sense whatsoever. Don't let them influence you--God doesn't!

In regard to spiritual matters, walk your talk. You'll have a much happier life, and so will the rest of us.

Relationships

Some of the most miserable people I know are very wealthy. Their misery comes from lousy relationships as they traded family for money.

~~~~~~
Anyone who neglects their family to get rich is a jerk.
~~~~~~

The man or woman who focuses on their beloved career while leaving the other parent to raise the kids is also a jerk (I have a stronger word in mind). Neglecting your family is the lowest form of cowardice, and it's rampant in our country. Pay attention to your people. (More on this in chapter ten.)

Where Do You Stand in Each Area?

The following diagram is called a Life Pie. The whole pie represents how you feel your whole life is shaping up. A slice of the pie represents a slice of life. Follow the instructions that follow the diagram to measure each of the five areas of your life. There's no judgment on how you measure yourself--no one else's opinion of where you stand matters. This is your honest opinion of *your* life.

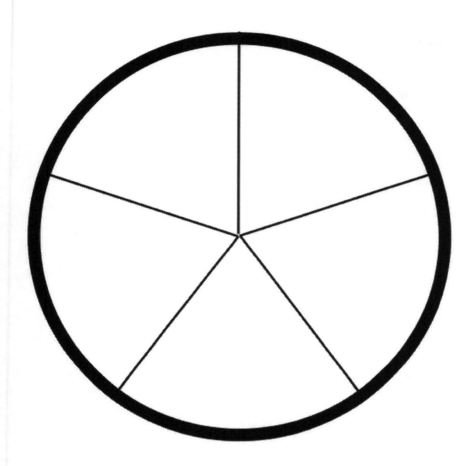

Health

How do you feel about your health? List the first three emotions that come up:

_____

_____

_____

Now score the following sub-areas of your health on a scale of zero-to-ten. A zero means you're extremely unhappy and a ten means you're completely satisfied.

Physically vital _____

Rarely ill _____

Weight under control _____

Mentally engaged _____

Spending less than a few minutes per day in negative emotional state (sad, angry, fearful, or disgusted) _____

Determine your score for this category by adding the scores and dividing the sum by 5 to get the average: ____

Add one point to the average if 2 of your 3 emotional words are positive. Deduct a point if you're experiencing 2 negatives of the 3 emotions.

Your health score _____.

Write HEALTH on one slice of the pie, draw a line across the section indicating your level of satisfaction. Consider a zero at the center point and a ten at the outer edge. A 3 would segment the narrowest third of the piece of pie, while a 6 or 7 would mark off about two-thirds from the center out. You're marking your level of satisfaction at 30, 40, 80, or whatever percent.

Shade in the health piece from zero to your mark. The white spaces indicate how much you believe you can grow.

Repeat the above steps for each category.

Wealth

How do you feel about your financial situation? List the first three emotions that come up:

_____

_____

_____

Now score the following sub-areas of your wealth using the same 0-10 scale.

Tracking expenses _____

Spending under control _____

Saving 10% or more of each paycheck _____

Investing _____

Additional earning potential (room for a side hustle) _____

Determine your score for this category by adding the scores and dividing the sum by 5 to get the average: ____

Add one point if 2/3 of your emotions are positive. Deduct a point if you're experiencing 2/3 negative emotions.

Your wealth score _____.

Mark one slice of the pie WEALTH and draw a line indicating your level of satisfaction.

Shade in the wealth piece.

Career

How do you feel about your career? List the first three emotions that come up:

_____

_____

_____

Now score the following sub-areas of your career using the same 0-10 scale.

Engagement _____

Compensation _____

Career Path _____

Loyalty to your employer _____

Sense of Purpose _____

Determine your score for this category by adding the scores and dividing the sum by 5 to get the average: ____

Add one point if 2/3 of your emotions are positive. Deduct a point if you're experiencing 2/3 negative emotions.

Your career score _____.

Mark one slice of the pie CAREER and draw a line indicating your level of satisfaction.

Shade in the career piece.

Spirituality

How do you feel about your spirituality? List the first three emotions that come up:

_____

_____

_____

Now score the following sub-areas of your spirituality using the same 0-10 scale.

Peace _____

Direction _____

Sense of awe/wonder/mystery _____

Belief in your future _____

Compassion for others _____

Determine your score for this category by adding the scores and dividing the sum by 5 to get the average: ____

Add one point if 2/3 of your emotions are positive. Deduct a point if you're experiencing 2/3 negative emotions.

Your spirituality score _____.

Mark a slice of the pie SPIRITUALITY and draw a line indicating your level of satisfaction.

Shade in the spirituality piece.

Relationships

How do you feel about your relationships? List the first three emotions that come up:

_____

_____

_____

Now score the following sub-areas of your relationships using the same 0-10 scale.

Significant other _____

Romance _____

Friends _____

Neighbors _____

Coworkers _____

Determine your score for this category by adding the scores and dividing the sum by 5 to get the average: ____

Add one point if 2/3 of your emotions are positive. Deduct a point if you're experiencing 2/3 negative emotions.

Your relationship score _____.

As you did for the others, label and mark the slice of the pie indicating RELATIONSHIPS and draw a line indicating your level of satisfaction.

Shade in the relationship piece.

Which Area Do You Want to Work On?

Most people, when asked where they'd like to start, default to the lowest area of satisfaction. I have found that to be a bad idea. It's better just to start with the one that most interests you.

Read in that area. Get advice in that area. Get your mind right in that area by building up your knowledge, positive attitude, and confidence. Write a goal in that area. Most of all, take action that heats up that area.

Work on it for three months, and then complete a new life pie to measure your progress. Too little progress? Apply more heat. Another area is too cool for your taste? Move the pot and apply heat.

Thinking about that one area, what would you like to achieve? Be very specific, not "lose weight" or "get out of debt" but "lose 10 lbs in six weeks" or "pay off the car in 24 months". (More on this in chapter 5.)

_____

_____

_____

Imagine your goal is to pay off the car loan. Let's say 24 months have gone by and you did it. You paid off your car loan. Close your eyes and really imagine it, soak it in for several minutes. See the car title free and clear in your name. Hear your family tell you how proud they are of you. Smell the soap and wax as you give your car a good cleaning. Imagine touching your checkbook knowing you never have to make another car payment. I'd ask how it tastes, but I don't want you licking your car--that's gross.

I do want you to write down the emotions you feel while imagining that car is paid off (or you've achieved whatever goal you set)..

_____

_____

_____

Revisit these feelings when you're tempted to do something that will move you away from your goal.

Next, write an action plan. What will you do first, second, third, etc? And when you will do each step.

_____ Start _____

_____ Start _____

_____ Start _____

_____ Start _____

_____ Start _____

_____ Start _____

_____ Start _____

_____ Start _____

_____ Start _____

_____ Start _____

The next chapter helps you to create the skill that multi-millionaires use to create fantastic success.

That's a fact,
Jack

2

POSITIVE ATTITUDE OR NEGATIVE LIFE

Watch the chapter 2 video at vimeo.com/253083827

The famous motivational speaker Zig Ziglar once said, "Your attitude determines your altitude." We all know people, however, who have a great attitude, but crashed. Was Zig wrong? Not all all. Even people with great attitudes occasionally fail, but they get back up faster, and that's the real cause of their success. People with a negative attitude get down and stay down. A positive attitude makes it easier to get back up after a setback (and often avoids the setback in the first place).

In this chapter, you will learn:

- How your brain reacts to a positive or negative attitude.
- The fastest way to have a better day every day.

How Your Brain Reacts to a Positive or Negative Attitude

It's amazing to watch a person's brain waves on a computer screen when their attitude is positive or negative. A positive attitude lights up the creative problem-solving parts of the brain. In the person I watched, the lights varied from bright yellow to white. They looked like Christmas lights; they even blinked! The negative areas were a blue tint, much dimmer, and the person's negative attitude caused activity in the brain areas associated with anger, fear, sadness, tension, and anxiety.

Think about that for a minute. A positive attitude activates the parts of your brain that solve problems. A negative attitude brings darkness and activates the parts that cause more problems.

You've heard of the *fight or flight* response, of course. It's really fight, flight, or freeze; named after the three actions our bodies take when fear and anxiety come up. You and I call it stress and worry, and we both know that state of mind is the pits. A positive attitude helps us relax and solve problems creatively.

~~~~~~

What happens when you relax? You solve problems and come up with great ideas more easily. And, my friend, that's what you're paid for.

~~~~~~

My step-mother had a bad attitude. She filled her mind with junk, gossiped about people at work, and, well, I think if she'd won the lottery, she'd have complained about the taxes. At the other extreme, I had an aunt who was the most positive person around. Even though my uncle was an alcoholic, my aunt never had a mean word to say, never complained, and always encouraged others. Which one would you have enjoyed knowing? Which one was more fun to be around? Which one had the better life? Aunt Jonnie won every contest.

The Fastest Way to Have a Better Day Every Day

When I was a little kid, Aunt Jonnie taught me how to have a better attitude: *"Be grateful, honey."* She probably said that while handing me a plate of homemade biscuits and gravy or a slice of her famous chocolate pie. Jonnie was a teacher and she knew exactly when to land a point. She'd grown up when times were harder and getting a biscuit, much less a slice of pie, was something for which one was grateful. By training my young mind to *be grateful, honey,* Aunt Jonnie did more to make sure I had a better day every day than any of my instructors.

People who complain have a bad attitude. They're ungrateful and enjoy life less. Perhaps they feel entitled to something. Research shows that ungrateful people have fewer friends and more health problems. They focus on the bad things. Therefore, their brains quickly identify the hard realities we all experience. They think they have more negatives, but they don't--they trained their brains to see them more often.

We can train our brains to default toward a bad attitude. We can adopt an ungrateful spirit and spread it around like fresh manure.

Such adaptability to train our brains toward negativity is *good* news. You see, if you can train your brain to have a bad attitude and to be ungrateful, you can also train it to be grateful and have a great attitude.

People who are grateful tend to have a better attitude and to be happier throughout the day. Their gratitude trains their brain to see more to be grateful for, which causes their brains to dump happy chemicals into their bloodstream. That, in turn, causes their bodies to take happier actions *like noticing more things to be grateful for.* Nice cycle, isn't it?

~~~~~~

The fastest way to train your brain to see more good stuff, be happier, and have a better attitude all around is to start everyday with gratitude.

~~~~~~

Tomorrow, wake up three minutes earlier than usual. Grab your coffee, or whatever, and find a quiet, comfortable place to sit.

Write down three things you're grateful for that you had a hand in. That last part of the sentence is the key. You may look outside and be grateful for the pretty clouds, but since you don't have a single thing to do with making the pretty clouds, your brain doesn't know what to do with that piece of gratitude, so out it goes with the rest of the trash your head picks up during the day. On the other hand, if you got a good night's sleep because you went to bed at a decent time, avoided too much booze (alcohol disturbs restful sleep), and bought yourself a nice pillow, then you had a big hand in getting some sleep.

When you're grateful for something you had a hand in, and you write it down, your brain dumps some happy chemicals into your bloodstream. They make you feel better, and they motivate you to do something good. Some researchers believe that little bump of happiness can last as long as two hours, and may help you overcome several stress-inducing annoyances during that time.

Over the next several weeks, as you practice writing down the three things you're grateful for, your brain will begin to notice more things that you did well. Those thoughts dump more happy chemicals.

~~~~~~

Be a good drug addict. Notice more to be grateful for and get little bumps of happy chemicals every few hours--enough to make your entire day go better.

~~~~~~

You'll enjoy a more relaxed day, which leads to a better attitude and more problems solved, and, perhaps, a raise! Yes, I am saying you can actually get paid for being more grateful. What are you waiting for?

Some of my clients have asked if they could do their gratitude journal at lunch. Of course they can, but they'd miss a happier, more productive morning. Your choice as always, but I do it first thing.

Do it every day, too. Never, never, never, skip a day. If you skip, your brain thinks you were kidding and that you prefer an ungrateful, negative attitude. Do it everyday and your brain starts to rewire itself to see what you want to see and to behave like you want it to behave.

Cool? It gets better. What you believe determines how you behave.

That's a fact,
Jack

3

YOU LACK CONFIDENCE BECAUSE YOU BELIEVE LIES

Watch the chapter 3 video at vimeo.com/253123755

One of the most amazing things I've learned from studying neuroscience is that our brains do not know the difference between belief and action. Aunt Jonnie liked to remind me that, "Whether you think you can or think you can't, you're right." Today, we can prove she was right.

In this chapter, you will learn:

- How to discover beliefs that limit your success.
- How to rewire your brain with new, empowering beliefs.

This is my favorite chapter. From this point on, your life will never be the same.

Today, you can shut up the inner critic, laugh at your mistakes and failures, overcome self-doubt, and build confidence. You will develop the same mindset that propels average people toward amazing success. Belief is the primary ingredient that separates average earners from those who take home multiple six-figures.

~~~~~~

Decision is belief, belief is action, and action reinforces belief. A vicious or lucrative cycle that we choose.

~~~~~~~~~~~~~~~~~~~~~~~~~~~~~~~~~~~~~~~

In your brain, any belief was created by a decision you made (decision is belief). And once a belief is held, the brain signals the body to act on that belief (belief is action). Once the action is taken, the brain filters out things that disagree with the belief and filters in things that agree, so the action taken reinforces the belief and the cycle repeats. Negative beliefs become fears, positive beliefs become empowering confidence. Negative beliefs are almost always lies, while positive beliefs are almost always true. I'll say more about each of these realities.

You were born with only two fears: fear of falling and fear of loud noises. As you grew, you learned to walk and run and you defeated the fear of falling. You learned that loud noises, while startling, almost never mean anything scarier than that someone dropped something. You defeated the fear of loud noises. You should, therefore, be fearless, but you're not (neither am I, although I'm pretty close).

You and I *decide* to fear things that might happen; but they almost never do. It makes sense to fear God, bad people, and things that lead to bad outcomes (drug deals and cigarettes, for instance). Yet, people worry and fret about things that almost never happen. That's because the large majority of our fears are false. F-E-A-R usually means False Evidence Appearing Real.

When someone tells you something false as though it were true, you call that a lie. We all decide to lie to ourselves, but I'm guessing none of us like it. In a moment, you'll know how to stop it.

Second, every belief leads the brain to dump chemicals into the bloodstream that cause the body to take action based on that belief. Because this happens instantly, we can state that belief is action.

~~~~~~

The moment you tell yourself a lie, your brain believes that lie is a goal (something you want), it releases chemicals into your body, and your body begins acting to prove the belief true. Even if it's a lie, your body tries to prove that lie true.

~~~~~~

Our brains are magnificent goal-achieving machines. They create filters that limit our ability to recognize anything that disagrees with our belief and highlight anything that agrees. All humans are biased toward their beliefs, which explains all the political and religious arguing we see.

Years ago, a client told me she had an easy time getting asked on dates, but she could not keep a relationship going for more than a couple years. She was bright, energetic, and beautiful enough to be paid as a model. For some reason, she kept attracting men who would mistreat her. She believed she was not good enough to date a nice man, so she settled for the abusive men she kept attracting.

In reality, it was worse than that. Her belief caused her to walk, talk, and stand in a way that attracted predators. Her body responded to the belief as though it were true. As she kept dating terrible men, she reinforced her belief that she was only worthy of terrible men.

It took a week to prove to her that her belief was a lie. Within a month, she met the man of her dreams and asked him out. They'd known each other for ten years, but she did not see him as a match because her brain filtered him out. Once she cleared the belief, her answer was there (he'd been there all along, of course), and she acted in a way consistent with her new belief that she was good enough. They've been happily married for years now, which changed her life, and she is today one of the happiest people I know. What changed first? Her belief.

Discover Beliefs that Limit Your Success

As a reminder, limiting beliefs, that inner critic's badgering about why you can't do the thing to get the life you want, come in three flavors. Comparison beliefs create false characterizations of others as somehow better than us. Such comparisons are impossible to defend logically because other people do not share your experiences, burdens, benefits, gifts, or talents.

Scarcity beliefs dangerously create a poverty mindset. We believe we do not have enough and create a world where all we see is what we lack.

I call the last category *Bogeyman Beliefs*. We create monsters out of luck, unseen enemies, demons, even God, and these nonexistent evils rule us from realms of superstition and dark caves of deceit.

This exercise offers a simple way to discover your limiting beliefs—the ones preventing you from having the life you want. Read each statement and reflect for only *a few seconds* on how much you believe it. Listen to your gut. If it kicks up a heavy, negative emotional response, then that's probably a limiting belief.

~~~~~~

It does not matter if you think the statement is rational, true or false for others, or only true sometimes, it only matters that you believe it is true for you.

~~~~~~

You may have heard a parent say it or an influential teacher or other authority. Maybe you've experienced it one time too many, now you find yourself saying it to other people. Who knows, you may have seen it in a movie and believed it about yourself. It doesn't matter from where it came. It only matters that you believe it.

Mark the statements that you believe. Don't overthink it. No one on my end will judge you for having limiting beliefs. *All sane people have limiting beliefs--it's the crazies who don't!*

From here, our work clears the limits. Once you have gone through the entire list and circled the ones that ring a bell, cross out all but the four that elicit the deepest emotional response. I probably forgot to list several; add anything you need to add.

Directions

1. Highlight all the beliefs that you hold.
2. Cross out all but the most powerfully emotional four.
3. Don't overthink it.

Comparison Beliefs

I'm not good enough.

I'm not original/creative enough.

I don't have anything to offer.

I'm not [smart, talented, funny, good looking, _____] enough.

I can't be happy until he/she changes.

It's hard for me to make friends.

Other people get all the breaks in life.

I can never show signs of weakness.

If people really knew me they wouldn't like me.

I'm too old/young.

I'm a fraud.

I shouldn't put my needs before anyone else's.

People won't buy my idea.

I should be doing more.

I'm not as sociable or friendly as most people.

I should be happy with what I have.

I should be more like (parent, sibling, friend).

They have [the "it" I secretly want] but I wouldn't want their life.

Not everyone is cut out for [success, fame, wealth, _____].

I can't depend on anyone.

I always have to work so hard while others have it easy.

If you want it done right, do it yourself.

I need to know what others think before I start.

Scarcity Beliefs

I can't afford it.

It's been done, no point in trying.

There's not enough time.

All the good men/women are taken.

I'm going to end up alone.

If it hasn't happened yet it never will.

It never happens for me.

This is a man's world.

Women/minorities/_____ get all the breaks these days.

I don't have time.

Money is hard to make.

I can't be happy until I have more [money, better health, love, time].

It's too late for me to…

I don't have the right skills to do it.

If I pursue what I really love, my relationships will suffer.

I'm not good with money.

I can't grow my business/income by that much.

The economy is bad.

The time isn't right to start a business/change jobs.

Jobs are hard to find.

There's a right way to do things and I can't find it.

Bogeyman Beliefs

I'm just not lucky.

Somehow, I'll screw it up.

I don't know what I want.

Money just slips away from me.

I can't change.

[God, Universe, Satan, Shiva, Allah, _____] is punishing me.

I don't know where to start.

I don't deserve [love, success, money, happiness].

I just can't.

Things will never work out for me.

This [negative thing] always happens to me.

There's nothing I can do about my [health, job, finances, relationship].

I shouldn't have to tell them what's bothering me.

I don't know how.

Money is the root of evil. It just creates bigger problems.

I can't lose weight.

People can't be trusted/aren't reliable.

It probably won't work out anyway.

I can't make a living doing what I really love to do.

I can't ask because people will say no and then they won't like me.

Good things happen but they never last.

Other limiting beliefs:

_____

_____

_____

_____

Rewire Your Brain with Empowering Beliefs

As the cycle of negative beliefs and reinforcing actions continues, your brain creates neural pathways. The brain loves to go fast. It creates neural pathways to speed up operations. Neural pathways are superhighways that speed information through the brain. When you observe something through your primary senses (sight, hearing, taste, smell, and touch) you feel an emotion that deepens those neural pathways like a rut in a well-traveled road.

The minute you adopt a new belief, your brain starts creating a new neural pathway--new wiring goes in and increases in size, making it easier for thoughts to travel along the path. The instant you call a limiting belief a lie, your brain starts breaking up the old neural wiring.

Your brain is built to wire and rewire as you decide to believe something, and this rewiring is surprisingly simple.

After studying neuroscience for a dozen years, reading books, hundreds of articles and studies, hearing academic lectures, interviewing several of the most noteworthy experts in the field (and hiring a few to coach me), I assure you that the science is real.

You can rewire your brain with new, empowering beliefs. How?

First, *believe it works*. You can read, study, interview, and hire the doctors, like I did, spending over 10,000 hours and $25,000, or you accept my word. Your choice.

~~~~~~

Until you stop believing lies that "you're just that way" and start believing the truth that you can rewire your brain, mindset programs won't work for you.

~~~~~~

Second, *you must want it*. Until you believe change is possible and you want to change, you won't. You'll make excuses, dream up new lies, and stay stuck in a meager existence (and you might even get worse because you're reinforcing negative beliefs).

~~~~~~

Nothing changes without believing it's possible and wanting it to happen. Remember that the next time you feel the need to change someone.

~~~~~~

For each of your four most powerful limiting beliefs, *decide* on a new belief. (Remember, a belief is a decision.) For instance, one of mine was

"God is punishing me." I know this is a lie because I have read the bible all the way through more than twenty times and it says *God is for us.* More importantly, I have seen God do things for people and me that defy the laws of physics, and can only be labeled miraculous. When I am honest, my life--from abuse and near homelessness to happily married 34+ years, kids who love, like, and respect me, 11 successful businesses, superior health, and deep spiritual understanding--I realized how silly it is to think anything other than that God is for me. But, I was lying to myself.

My truthful, new decision was "God is for me." Everything changed as I rewired my brain to see all the things God does to prove his love, and those are things I write in my gratitude journal every morning.

You will see a brief worksheet at the end of this chapter. Write your new, empowering decisions/beliefs in the left column. Over the next week, write evidence that proves the new belief true. Include those in your daily gratitude journal as well.

Soon, you'll notice more evidence for your new beliefs. Eventually, you will hardly remember your old, limiting beliefs at all.

Like a water filter, your brain will filter in clean beliefs, filter out the dirt and poison, and your body will take different actions. You will show up differently. Your friends and family may notice, and they may even criticize you because, sadly, people with limiting beliefs do not like to be around empowered people. I've found that most people believe it is us who make them feel they're trapped in a miserable state of mind while we're easily roaming free. People will often blame anything but the real cause for their problems, don't you agree?

The process of creating empowering beliefs may cause some temporary pain. You may learn who your real friends are--they're the ones who empower you and celebrate your new beliefs and positive attitude.

~~~~~~

Enemies want you limited. Friends want you empowered.

~~~~~~

Repeat your new beliefs every morning, right after you complete your gratitude journal. Repeat them again at lunch, and one more time at dinner. Repeating them aloud is better than silently, and silently is better than not at all. Repeating them 100 times is better than fifty, and one time is better than none. Don't forget: you *decide* to believe.

My Empowering Beliefs   **Evidence Proving Them True**

1.

2.

3.

4.

In the next chapter, we will begin training your brain by envisioning what the good life means to you. Vision is like your personal map to wherever you want your life to go.

That's a fact,
Jack

4

LACK OF VISION CAN SMACK YOUR FACE INTO A POLE

Watch the chapter 4 video at https://vimeo.com/253069998

Last week, I saw a guy walk into a light pole. He was walking while looking at his phone. In a sense, he lacked proper vision, don't you agree? He was walking the right right way, the wrong way.

Have you ever taken the wrong road? I was driving to Ft. Worth one time, but I took the wrong road and ended up in Dallas. Dallas is a nice place, but I wanted to be somewhere else.

Trying to guide a life (or a business) without a clear vision of where you want to go pretty much guarantees you'll end up somewhere else. People who lack vision run into the wrong things. In this chapter, you will learn:

- The amazing power of a clear vision for you and the people closest to you.
- How to find your vision for your life.

Now that you know what beliefs held you back all these years, you're ready to imagine a better destination. My clients often say this is the easiest lesson. It's literally day dreaming your way to a better life.

The Amazing Power of a Clear Vision

Most of the time, when we ask someone, "What do you want to do?" or "Where would you like your life to go?" they lock up and cannot think of anything specific. My guess is that's changed since you were five. Back then, someone asked and you probably had an answer. What changed?

Your beliefs changed.

I've found that most people get stuck because they either believe they should wow me with their answer or that by answering at all, they're committing to something they may not want later. Neither is true, but as adults, most of us find ourselves limited by beliefs of what we "should be" instead of what we want to be. We didn't have that problem as kids--we decided to believe it. Say this out loud, "I WILL STOP SHOULDING ON MYSELF!" (Smile, you know that's funny.)

What most people learned since kindergarten is to stop dreaming, to stop having a vision of where they want to go. Weak vision means not knowing what to do, and that leads to a place you probably didn't want to go. Sadly, this weak vision not only holds most people back from getting the life they want, it holds their loved ones back as well. Your family sees you struggling without a clear destination, and they begin to think that's the way life is supposed to work.

It's like watching someone without a map keep getting lost and deciding, "Well, we aren't where we thought we were going. I guess we'll just stay here." People can't help but influence the people closest to them. Years later, when someone asks the adult child of visionless parents where they want to go, the person thinks, "Mama and Daddy never talked about vision. Maybe it's not something for people like us."

~~~~~~

Unclear, weak vision is contagious.

~~~~~~

Many studies have shown the power of parents and peer groups. Many people remember a parent or grandparent telling them not to hang around with certain kids. My grandmother and grandfather often told me to be careful hanging around some of the kids I liked hanging around. Papa said, "Those boys don't know where they're headed." Mema was even more blunt, "Those kids will bring you down, baby." A man or woman of vision can spot its lack. My first coach was also a man of vision who told me, "Take a look at your five closest friends. In five years, your life will look like theirs." That was bad news for me because my five closest friends were going nowhere fast--they had no vision at all for going where I wanted to go.

Do yourself and your family a favor. Develop a clear vision.

How to Find Your Vision for Your Life

Let's answer the question in an easier way. Get specific as you can when thinking through each element. Write yourself a letter.

~~~~~~

What, to you, does it feel like to have the good life? Vision makes you feel something. What's it looks like? You see something, too.

~~~~~~

Seriously, write a letter to you in the future. Cast your vision out ten or twenty years. How's your health? What are you doing for a living, and how much meaning does your work add to your life. What's your income? How much wealth have you built and how did you do it? Where have you traveled and what's your favorite vacation spot? What do you do for fun and with whom? Talk a bit about your best relationships. Who's made the journey through time with you, who hasn't, and what makes the special relationships extraordinary? Where do you live and what's your house like? Describe your spiritual life, and how it empowers other areas.

Start with some basic opinions of what the good life means to you. Then write your letter.

To me, good health means _____

_____

For me, having satisfying relationships means _____

_____

In my opinion, having a meaningful career means _____

_____

I believe an empowering spiritual life means _____

_____

To me, this is enough wealth: $_____.00

Letter to Me on (future date) _____
Written [today]

_____

_____

_____

_____

_____

_____

_____

_____

_____

You may need some more paper. Go for it!

The more specific your letter, the greater the emotional response. The greater the emotional response, the more your brain will retain the vision and work for it.

Want to help your loved ones get a vision? Go way out on a limb and share your letter. I know it takes courage, but you're no longer held back by a limiting belief in timidity are you? Amp it up.

This exercise trains your brain to see a vision for your life. By telling others your vision, you build for them an idea of where they can go if they go with you.

~~~~~~

Vision really helps if you run an organization. It helps people opt in and remain loyal or opt out and, therefore, not crater your company.

~~~~~~~~~~~~~~~~~~~~~~~~~~~~~~~~~~~~~

Read your letter over and over again. Condense it into one overarching sentence. It may take you awhile. Do it anyway. It's easier if you read your letter slowly, out loud, and give yourself time to soak in the meaning.

I see my good life, and it looks like _____

_____

_____

Now, imagine you already have it. Allow the joy of those accomplishments to sink in until you can hear the sound of your loved ones thanking you, see the fantastic doctor's report on your robust health, smell smoke as you burn the mortgage on your paid off home, and the leather seats on your new car (the one you paid cash for), feel the sense of power from a vibrant, sensible spirituality. Let all that sink in for ten or fifteen minutes.

Every morning, read your vision statement. Every week, read the letter. If anything needs to change, change it, but don't back down. Don't let the inner critic get hold of it.. Relax and envision life as you want it.

As you begin your day, you're now programming your mind to filter in things that will get you to the life you envision. By believing and repeating your vision, you will also filter out the things that used to take you off track. The distractions of old hurts, and new, shiny objects that do not feed your vision will eventually become relics of the past.

One of my clients says the old elephants have become like gnats. They're still around, but instead of stomping and crushing her dreams, they're just annoying and she swats them away.

~~~~~~

As you think about the day ahead, envision opportunities, appointments, errands, problems you will solve, people you will serve, and how you want the day to go. Envision a perfect day.

~~~~~~

If anything comes along that starts stressing you out, stop and take a deep breath. Remind yourself that today is a perfect day. Remember where your life is headed, and that setbacks almost always teach you something important. If not, then they're just gnats along the road to the good life you envision.

The next chapter uses your vision to create goals. You will use goals to go out there and grab the good life.

That's a fact,
Jack

5

PEOPLE WHO SET GOALS DON'T GET IT ALL BUT THEY GET MORE THAN PEOPLE WHO DON'T

Watch the chapter 5 video at https://vimeo.com/253127124

Research shows that not everyone who sets goals reaches all the goals they set. That's not the whole story, however. Research also shows that people who set goals tend to accomplish more than people who don't.

Creating your best life is a goal, and to get there, you will need hundreds of small goals along the way. In this session, you will learn:

- The best way to set a goal.
- How to track progress toward a goal.
- What to do when you find things or people taking you away from your goal.

The Best Way to Set a Goal

Let's revisit: *any belief you hold is interpreted as a goal by your brain.* You're creating goals everytime you decide to believe something, which we learned can work against you.

Many people believe, for instance, that they're good singers and the truth matters not one bit. Their brains filter out evidence of bad singing and filter in evidence that they're the next Adele. This phenomenon explains the try out portion of shows like *American Idol.* Some poor kid has listened to their parents and their church telling them they can sing, when all of America knows they really can't. Mama and the preacher weren't intentionally lying, they were being kind trying to spare the feelings of a loved one.

People who make a living selling recordings and television shows featuring great singers have different goals. They want nothing but real, salable talent. They choose not to be so kind. They slam the kid's dream against the rocks of reality. Dashed dreams are not fun--we've all seen the arguing and wailing that accompany the truth.

~~~~~~
You already have many goals; they're your beliefs.
~~~~~~

Too often, you and I see a bad singer's belief overwhelm common sense and mountains of evidence. The same is true with a belief when the belief is a lie. Setting goals based on lies leads to misery.

Because such an emotional meltdown is extremely unpleasant, let's set goals based on truth. The best goal connects to one of your current, truthful beliefs.

If nobody wants to pay you for singing, you probably aren't that good. What do they pay you for? That's a good place to create a goal to get better at that thing. When you're good enough, you become known for it. When you're known for it, people hunt you down and pay you much more than average to do it.

There are seven steps to setting a good goal. In this exercise we will use *getting a promotion at work* for the example. I've found career goals to be the most commonly malformed and, therefore, underachieved of goals. In a minute, you'll know why a bad goal makes something like a promotion almost impossible to achieve.

We can easily remember the steps using the acronym SMART-PC:

- Specific
- Measurable
- Attainable
- Reasonable
- Time bound
- Positive
- Controllable

Specific

Our brains love specificity. The brain does not know what to do with a vague goal. Every night while you're sleeping, your brain is working, filing and sorting the various things you learned that day. The vague goal goes out with the rest of the trash. *I will get that promotion* almost never causes someone to actually get promoted; it's unspecific.

A specific goal might be: "I will advance to [Sales Manager and please fill in whatever title you prefer] by [learning everything about our products and the best sales tactics, and by outworking everyone in my office]." That's more specific, and the brain immediately starts working in the direction of finding product manuals, books, podcasts, and anything else necessary to hit that goal. It's still not enough.

Measurable

The goal needs a measurement to kick the brain into a higher gear. "I will increase my sales 10% per month until I lead the entire company by studying my craft daily and staying at the office an hour longer than the top three sales people." Now it includes measures. It's still a lousy goal.

Attainable

Let's say the author of the above goal is a married woman with a two-year-old, which is not uncommon for younger sales women. She can't hit the goal because staying late everyday is unattainable (we can assume that she is the kind of honorable woman who values a relationship with her child as well as her work).

A friend of mine realized (when his wife left him) that his work life had gotten out of bounds. He wanted the promotion and healthy relationships, so he set a goal to win back his family by taking a month off to travel with them, then he would get back to his 70-hour work week. He failed as soon as he told his wife the grand plan. Of course he failed, his brain knew that goal was unattainable without her buy-in, and she was not about to agree to single parenting. He sabotaged the effort.

An attainable goal makes sense. Smaller, attainable goals often result in success more often than large goals because they make sense. An attainable goal might look like: "I will increase my sales 10% per month until I lead the entire company by studying my craft daily, making five more calls per week than the top three sales people, and getting support from my family." It still needs work.

Reasonable

An unreasonable goal conflicts with other goals. Adding to our story, we notice that our soon to be Sales Manager friend has another goal to gain her family's support in her career, which is brilliant. Many successful people realize that immediate family makes a perfect band of sharp accountability partners and involve them in career and wealth-building goals. Too many achievers fall under the temptation to go it alone only to find their closest allies departed.

Adjust the goal to be more reasonable. Perhaps this: "I will increase my sales 10% per month until I lead the entire company by studying my craft daily, making five more calls per week than the top three sales people, and getting my family's support by communicating my plans and progress and asking for their honest feedback."

Time bound

We're almost done. By placing a time limit on the goal, we create a sense of urgency in the brain. That magnificent brain of yours will take larger and more concrete action on an urgent goal. The next revision: "I will become Sales Manager in two years by increasing my sales 10% per month until I lead the entire company by studying my craft daily, making five more calls per week than the top three sales people make, and by getting my family's support by communicating my plans and progress and asking for their honest feedback." Add two checks and you're done.

Positive

Our brains prefer positive statements. The goal qualifies as written, but one nuance will make it even better. I've found that the phrase *I decide* carries more power than *I will*. Our new version reads: *I decide to become Sales Manager in two years by increasing my sales 10% per month until I lead the entire company by studying my craft daily, making five more calls per week than the top three sales people make, and by getting my family's support by communicating my plans and progress and asking for their honest feedback.*

Controllable

Take a look at the goal and make sure that every part of it is under the goal setter's control. *I decide to become Sales Manager in two years by increasing my sales 10% per month until I lead the entire company by studying my craft daily, making five more calls per week than the top three sales people make, and by getting my family's support by communicating my plans and progress and asking for their honest feedback.* Is anything in that goal outside the person's control?

Yes! She cannot control her boss's decision to promote her even if she's the best person for the next management opening. Nor can she control when the Sales Manager position comes open (pulling a Tonya Harding on the current Sales Manager is not an option for ethical people like us). If we assume the person will become Sales Manager at her present company, her goal is out of her control. If, however, she and her familial accountability partners are open to a move, then she's back in control. If it's controllable, it's a good goal.

What of they are not open to a move? One assumes there are other companies in this woman's town, or she may extend the timeline out another year, wait and see, and make an adjustment if necessary. A goal is not written in stone. Change it when circumstances change.

Often, circumstances and parameters for a goal change in unexpected ways. A client tried to set a goal to make her husband come to church with her. Bad idea because that's not something she could control without causing a bigger problem. Very few churches allow women to bring their husbands in under duress. She had to let him come along of his own free will, which is exactly how God treats us, by the way. Her goal might've been a good one if she wanted to be known as a nagging church lady, which she did not.

Instead, she set the goal of gaining so much value and becoming such a positive, productive, peaceful person from her church-going, that her life would be as attractive to her husband as a porch light to a moth. That was years ago, and I still smile when I think about the results.

After a month, she changed churches because, she said, "I realized my church was full of grumps. No wonder my husband doesn't want to go!" (May she influence multitudes!)

By the end of a month at the new church, her husband noticed how cheerful she was when she got home. The next Sunday, he asked if he could drive her and said, "I'll sit in the back so when it's over we can beat the traffic out of there." Evidently, he found out why she was so pleasant, and he joined the church a couple weeks later. A good goal often produces many good results.

Good goals predict good stuff happening. Set a SMART-PC goal in each of the five areas of your life.

My health goal: _____

_____

_____

_____

My wealth goal: _____

_____

_____

_____

My career goal: _____

_____

_____

_____

My relationship goal: _____

_____

_____

_____

My spiritual goal: _____

_____

_____

_____

Track Progress Toward a Goal

If your goal is small, tracking progress may not matter. For instance, if someone sets a goal to read a book in one week and it's a small book like this one, then they know to read about twelve pages each day. Just look at the page numbers every day. That's keeping track.

What if the goal is to *write* a book, even a very brief book like this one? That's a bit more complex, isn't it?

~~~~~~

To tackle a big goal requires a more complex tracking system.

~~~~~~

Things like building a house, graduating college, writing a book, or starting a business have dozens of steps and often take more than a year to achieve. I like a visual system to track more complex goals.

Type out all the steps necessary to achieve the goal, one step per line. You may have hundreds of steps. I built houses for many years, and this systems worked magnificently to tracks the hundreds of steps from creating architectural drawings, through various construction phases, and all the way to handing the keys to my customer. Type or write out your steps and print it all. Tape the pages together, and hang the whole thing horizontally on the wall. The various steps will read vertically like the titles on book spines lined up on a shelf.

Highlight the big milestones (for a college degree, it might be semesters completed and for a book, that might be the chapter titles). Write a date on each step indicating when you believe you can complete that step. Dates may change down the line if something does not happen on time. Don't beat yourself up if you miss a deadline, just write in new due dates and keep plugging along.

Tack a piece of string tightly along the top of the papers from one side to the other. Cut another, footlong piece of string and tie a paperclip at each end. Hang one paperclip on the horizontal string stretching across your timeline of steps, and let the other paperclip act as a weight to keep the vertical string straight. As you complete a task, slide the vertical string along the horizontal string to show progress on tasks.

The visual reminder of where one is in the process tends to motivate them to keep going. To stay on track, they might need to work an evening or a weekend. Or, they may get ahead, and enjoy some time off. Either way, they know.

If you look online, you'll find several software packages that build a similar type of chart that helps you keep a goal on track. I like the paper and string method for a couple reasons: it works and it's cheap! I used it to build a successful construction business that delivered projects on time. I used it again to finish a doctoral dissertation in record time. Most people like the visual reminder because our brains enjoy visual clues. But the choice is yours.

What to Do When Things or People Stagnate Progress

If you're consistently getting off track, it's time for some soul-searching. Do you really want this goal? If so, is a limiting belief sabotaging your effort?

Is your family taking you away from your dream? That's a tough realization. It happened to me in college, again in my first business, and again in grad school. I had to explain to my Dad that for a few years, my goal was going to take up more of my time, and he would get less of me. I would not be at every family function, but I would make all the important holidays and a few other events.

~~~~~~
Achieving a goal means letting other things go.
~~~~~~

Friend time can be tougher to let go than family time. Real friends cheer us to greater heights. People masquerading as friends prefer their own goals to ours. Fake friends pester you to go to big party the night before an important presentation. Your real friends push you to stay home and do your work, encouraging greater success.

~~~~~~

Sometimes, we have to face the fact that our friends are not really our friends. Our real friends want the best for us.

~~~~~~

If you find things taking you away from your goal, let the things go or change your goal. If you find people taking you away from your goal, kiss them or your goal goodbye. You can't have both.

With all these great goals, you may experience some time pressure. Something has to give to get what you want, right? The next chapter examines time management.

That's a fact,
Jack

6

YOU HAVE ALL THE TIME YOU NEED, BUT YOU'RE A LOUSY INVESTOR

Watch the chapter 6 video at https://vimeo.com/253129916

Think of someone you admire who is wildly successful. Guess what? You have exactly the same amount of time every week that they have: 168 hours. The difference is that they invest and manage time better than most people do, and you can fix that by managing your time more wisely.

In this chapter, you'll learn two old tricks to manage new time.

- The best time management idea of all time.
- A simple trick with a tomato to do more in less time.

The Best Time Management Idea of All Time

Imagine getting paid $400,000 for a single idea that takes less than five minutes to explain. The dean of my college told me a story about a guy named Ivy Lee. Mr. Lee was a businessman in the early part of the 20th Century. He was summoned to the office of the president of a large steel company with an invitation to offer a good idea.

When Mr. Lee walked in the man's office, he asked for a few minutes with each of the company's executives to teach them a simple trick to get more of the right things done each day. No more of the president's valuable time would be required. The president is reported to have asked how much this idea would cost, and Mr. Lee replied something to the effect of: "Nothing now. Try it for three months and send me a check for whatever you think it's worth."

When Mr. Lee met with each executive, he removed an index card from his coat pocket. He placed the card on the executive's desk and said, more or less, this:

> *Before you leave work today, write the six most important things you want to do tomorrow on that card. Do not write more than six items.*
>
> *Go home, enjoy your family, and get a good night's sleep. When you return to your office in the morning, start in on item number one.*
>
> *Do item one until you either can do no more or you have completed it. Then, and only then, move on to item two. Do not start on item three until item two is either completed or stalled beyond your control. Continue as such through the list. At the end of the day, make a new list.*
>
> *That idea will make you money by focusing your energy on the single, most important task at all times. Please call if I may be of further service.*

The story goes that three months later, the company president, Charles Schwab of Bethlehem Steel, who was at that time one of the wealthiest men in the world, sent Mr. Lee a check for $25,000, which is worth about $400,000 in today's money. It is claimed that Mr. Schwab credited Ivy Lee's time management system as the greatest single idea he ever heard. And, as you might have guessed, Mr. Lee did a great deal more business with Mr. Schwab and many other people over the next several years.

The brilliance of the idea lies in its simplicity. It forces action. It forces focus onto one thing and one thing only. It prevents distraction and procrastination. It enabled decisiveness. All these are disciplines that the most successful people use to get more done in a single day than most people do in a week. Try it.

Write a prioritized list of the six most important things to do. Do the first to completion, then tackle the second, and so on.

A Simple Trick with a Tomato to Get More Done

My second favorite time management idea is called the Pomodoro Technique, named after a kitchen timer. In the 1980s, Francesco Cirillo was a consultant experimenting with various time management techniques. He found that by setting a timer for twenty-five minutes followed by a five minute break, he maintained his focus and produced better work than if he tried working longer or avoiding breaks.

After many experiments, the twenty-five minutes on, five minutes off routine produced the best results. To keep track, he used a kitchen timer that was shaped like a tomato. *Pomodoro* is Italian for "tomato," thus the name. (To keep myself on track, I bought a $5 timer shaped like a tomato with a happy little face drawn on it. My wife liked my little tomato so much that she borrowed it from me permanently. I bought another one shaped like a happy little onion. She isn't as fond of onions.)

Cirillo's experiment did not simply involve a timer and an amount of time. For twenty-five minutes, he did only one thing. No phone, no interruptions whatsoever. Work only on one thing and only for twenty-five minutes.

During his break, he did not answer messages. He took a brief walk, talked to a colleague, or went to the bathroom. I imagine his advice today would allow a few minutes on Facebook or web surfing, but only for five minutes, and really, it would be much better for one's health to take a walk and save Facebook for later, unless you're stopping to post an insight from this book (smile).

~~~~~~

Spend no more than 25 minutes on a task with no distractions. Take a 5 minute break. Then another 25 minute work session followed by a break, and so on through the day. 25:5:25:5... You'll get more done.

~~~~~~

In our previous chapter, you learned to set goals. Watch what happens when you list the tasks associated with achieving your goals as the six items on your index card. Then see if a focused twenty-five minutes of work on one item plows you through that list faster and better than ever. I've found that these two techniques work, and hundreds of my clients agree: *they'll work for you too.*

Even with frequent breaks, our energy drains at the end of the day. Sometimes, things happen that cause energy to be low at the beginning of the day. Our next chapter discusses energy management.

That's a fact,
Jack

7

ENERGY MANAGEMENT: YOUR BRAIN IS LIKE A BATTERY

Watch the chapter 7 video at https://vimeo.com/253132229

You know how at the end of some days you feel like you really got a lot done, and other days it feels like you worked all day but nothing got done? To have your best life means not only getting things done that energize you, but also limiting things that drain your energy.

~~~~~~

Because the brain is like a battery, it only has so much energy before it needs to rest. Opening too many draining tasks, like open apps on your phone, drains the brain-battery faster.

~~~~~~

In this chapter, you will learn:

- How to find your energy drains.

- How to know what adds energy to your day.
- How to manage your day to get more gains and fewer drains.

Find Your Energy Drains

Finding what drains you is, admittedly, a bit draining. To get the most complete understanding of your drains means carrying around a little notebook and jotting down every time you find yourself doing a task or contemplating a task that triggers a negative emotional state. Consider carrying this book around and use the form below.

~~~~~~

The draining emotions--fear, anger, disgust, and sadness--are there to protect us. They're not there to bathe in.

~~~~~~

We've learned the mindset training tactic of switching from a negative belief to its positive opposite, but sometimes that's extremely difficult if you're consistently upset by a particular task. It helps to take all the notes you can on those negativity triggering, draining tasks.

Keep the list for a week. Look over your complete list, counting which items come up most frequently. List those in order of their frequency. Those are your drains.

Know What Adds Energy to Your Day

Make a similar list of tasks that you love doing. Energizing tasks seem to make time stand still. You feel better while doing them and get a big boost when you complete one.

It's more efficient to make both lists at the same time. If you make your own list, put a small negative symbol (-) in front of the draining tasks and a positive symbol (+) in front of your gains.

Take a look at both lists side by side. Look for patterns. Do some things give you energy in the morning, but doing the same task drains you in the afternoon? This is surprisingly common. As the day wears on, our brains get tired just like our feet do. Something that might be fun in the morning becomes pure drudgery by 3:00 PM.

Below, you will see a table to list your energy gains and drains. It helps to write things down and update the list each day for about a week as you find more.

Gains

Tasks that energize me:

_____

_____

_____

_____

_____

_____

_____

_____

_____

_____

People who energize me:

_____

_____

_____

_____

Drains

Tasks that drain my energy:

_____

_____

_____

_____

_____

_____

_____

_____

_____

_____

_____

People who drain my energy:

_____

_____

_____

_____

_____

Manage Your Day to Get More Gains and Fewer Drains

The five minute break we learned in the pomodoro time management technique is a great way to give your brain some needed rest throughout the day. By taking breaks, you'll find yourself accomplishing more.

Another tactic to try is to arrange tasks so that those that give you energy in the morning are batched together to be completed in the morning. Similarly, schedule time in the afternoon to do tasks that add to your energy at that time of day.

As much as possible, offload tasks that drain you and spend more time doing tasks that add to your energy. Hire an assistant who enjoys doing the things that drain you. Or, you may be able to find a buddy at work, or a family member at home who enjoys doing something that drains you. Similarly, they may have a task they hate but you love. *Trade!*

~~~~~~

All this arranging and rearranging tasks can itself become a draining task. Learn to delegate.

~~~~~~

The best way to manage your energy is to switch from that miserable state where your negative emotions are in control to a creative state where joy is driving you throughout the day. Remember the chapter on beliefs? That's where you learned to decide to believe something new, something that makes you feel better about the task at hand.

Let say you hate folding clothes. The clothes still need to be folded, but imagine that you feel as though everyone forces you to fold clothes, and you're tired of it. See how quickly the belief that your family is taking advantage of you, not pitching in, and forcing you to do another chore puts you in a state of misery? You become angry that it's always you folding the dang clothes. Then you become sad that no one cares about your needs. Misery. Yuck.

Get out of that state quick! Perhaps you cannot trade folding clothes for a chore you enjoy. Okay, figure out what's making you sad or angry. There's a belief lurking down there, telling you something. Is it true? Probably not. It's highly unlikely that your family members are meeting behind your back to make your life miserable. *Cinderella* was fiction, remember? More likely, you've latched onto something that's not true and it's guiding you into a miserable hole.

Flip it. Remind yourself that you like your clothes neatly folded so they all fit where they're supposed to go, and so that they look fresh when you wear them. Tell yourself that nobody is better than you at folding clothes, and your family looks better because you fold clothes so well. Think about the discipline that folding clothes encourages--you're not a slob, you're sharp, put together, and professional! Whatever it takes to make yourself laugh and enjoy the time. Shoot, folding clothes may be one of the few times you get to be alone and think deep thoughts about your life. The point is to flip yourself out of misery and into joy as fast as possible.

Staying in misery creates stress. The next chapter helps you manage stress.

That's a fact,
Jack

Jack M. Allen, Ph.D.

.

.

8

STRESSED OUT OR OUT OF STRESS

Watch the chapter 8 video at https://vimeo.com/253134966

Despite what some may say, stress is here to stay. The question is how you will manage the normal stress of family life, work life, paying the bills, controlling spending, finding time to exercise, and doing all the other stuff you know you need to do but can't quite get done. Stress does not have to win. You can get out of it.

In this chapter, you will learn:

- What stress is.
- When stress is helpful.
- How to limit the negative effects of stress.

What Stress Is

Most of the time, when you or I talk about stress, we mean the bad kind. We refer to our lives as *stressful* or *stressed out,* meaning we don't know how much more of this we can take!

Once again, remember, *every thought causes the brain to dump chemicals into the bloodstream.* Those chemicals can calm us down or throw us into a rage, make us laugh or cry, put us to sleep or amp us up. Thoughts cause stress.

~~~~~~

Stress is the body's natural response to a thought. Good or bad stress results from good or bad thoughts.

~~~~~~

Stress is only bad when we get too much negative stress. Too much of those chemicals and the body starts to poison itself. Too much negative stress causes the brain to limit choices and often causes people to make bad choices. People under extreme stress become violent more easily and often turn to drugs or alcohol to reduce their stress. You've probably known someone who "worried her/himself sick," got so angry they had a heart attack, or was so overwhelmed by stress that they became addicted to drugs or alcohol, which caused more stress.

When Stress is Helpful

Not all stress is bad. The runner fidgets around on the track, trying to stay loose and calm, and the starter yells, "On your marks!"

Immediately, the runner's body responds with stress. The runner thinks, "The race is about to start. All my training goes into this moment." They kneel down, put their feet in the blocks, and their whole body tenses, waiting for the call: "Set" and the starting gun to go! That's stress! It's the good kind. It causes us explode into a task we enjoy whether it's a sporting event, painting, or the start of a movie we've been looking forward to seeing. Remember the stress you felt on your first day at your job? That was probably good stress.

~~~~~~

Good stress causes attention to sharpen and all the senses to heighten.

~~~~~~

It makes us do more in less time with better results. Good stress results from thinking positively about the process and outcomes of a task.

How to Limit the Negative Effects of Stress

If you approach a task while thinking about how hard it is or how much you fear messing it up, you'll soon be under bad stress. On the other hand, if you think about what you'll learn, increasing your skill everytime you tackle that task, and the pleasure you'll feel when it's complete, your brain will send good chemicals through your body and you'll be under good stress.

~~~~~~

Stress management is all about controlling your thoughts.

~~~~~~

It really is about that simple. Our beliefs exercise in chapter three helps you train your brain to be more in control of your thoughts. If you're still struggling, repeat that chapter. Many of my clients repeat chapter three several times.

Breathing deeply offers another helpful tactic. I've found that taking three or four deep breaths, inhaling and exhaling slowly and controlled helps. Studies show that deep breathing begins calming a person's heart rate within thirty seconds.

You've probably heard of meditation. Meditation is proven to reduce stress. Check out YouTube for free instructional videos on meditation techniques. I've found that simply sitting in a comfortable chair in a quiet room, feet on the floor, hands in my lap, eyes closed, breathing deeply while paying attention to nothing but my breathing--inhale, exhale, slowly, under control, inhale, exhale, inhale, exhale. It's surprisingly calming, and the calm feeling lasts several hours. When a stray thought comes up, even if it's negative, just let it pass like a car going by in the street: there it is and there it goes.

Prayer is also proven to calm stress. I've found that prayer and meditation both work to reduce stress so, I do both.

~~~~~~

The difference between prayer and meditation is that prayer is filling the mind with good thoughts while meditation is emptying the mind of all thoughts. Both work.

~~~~~~

With practice, we can manage stress. Doing so provides incredible health and spiritual benefits. Gaining control of stress helps every area of life, and your family will be happier too because you won't be so freaking stressed out!

The next chapter deals with something that causes way too much stress in way too many people. Money management often confuses us with it's apparent complexity, but it's really as easy as one plus one equals two.

That's a fact,
Jack

9

POVERTY IS BAD MONEY MANAGEMENT

Watch the chapter 9 video at https://vimeo.com/253136809

We all know that someone should have taught us how to manage money back in high school, but that rarely happened.

In this chapter, you will learn:

- How to manage money.
- How to stop worrying about money.

How to Manage Money

Money is not, like some people think, the root of all evil. That quote is often attributed to the bible, but if you look it up, it really says: *The love of money is the root of evil,* which makes a ton of sense, doesn't it? A person who loves money will do just about anything to get more, including hurt others.

~~~~~~

Use money and love people. Do not love money and use people.
Simple, isn't it?

~~~~~~

Money gives us more choices. Managing money is as easy as managing choices.

With more money, we have more options for housing, clothing, education, food, health care, recreation, the list is endless, isn't it? Because the choices money provides increase with the more money one has, people often get jealous of those with more because they focus on the lack of choices they have. That's a dead end game creating several limiting beliefs in the categories of comparison and scarcity. Because someone will always have more money and choices than you do does not make you less valuable. Such jealousy does nothing but cause stress, and stress causes us to make poor choices with everything, especially our money.

Instead, wouldn't it be better to calmly manage your money like you manage your thoughts and your stress?

If you find money woes stressing you out and you would prefer to rid yourself of that stress, you'll need to change some habits. The first is your tracking system for expenses. I've found that not tracking expenses is like being in a boat that leaks and not finding the hole. Sooner or later, that boat will sink, unless you plug the hole. Tracking expenses shows you exactly where the hole is, and it becomes your choice to plug it or let it continue to leak.

~~~~~~

Manage money by tracking what comes in and what goes out. Yes, it's a pain, but it beats the stress of wondering if you have enough money.

~~~~~~

If you've had a tough time managing money, please start on the bonus reading list at the back of this book. *Total Money Makeover* has helped millions of people manage their money, get out debt, and start building wealth. *Rich Dad, Poor Dad* helps create a wealth mindset by understanding how money works. *The Investor's Manifesto* offers simple guidance on investing. Reading all three means first investing in yourself, which always pays quick dividends that last.

~~~~~~

Invest in yourself first. It's the only investment I've found with a guaranteed high rate of return.

~~~~~~

Managing money is really as simple as adding and subtracting. Once you know your total income and expenses, subtract expenses from income. If the amount is greater than zero, put that into savings until you have a couple months of expenses saved. Any savings beyond that can go into an investment that pays more interest.

If the sum is less than zero, start cutting expenses. Cutting expenses is the fastest way to have more money to manage. Most often, when someone is spending more than they earn, we find three thieves robbing them and all three are in the entertainment business. Restaurants, especially fast food restaurants, cost three to ten times more than eating at home or taking your lunch to work. I know it's a pain to cook all the time, so is being broke.

Second, cable and satellite television packages are fun and entertaining, and they erode your paycheck. Entertaining library books are free.

~~~~~~

If you want to be wealthy, make the hard choices that wealthy people make. Let your investments pay for pleasure. This usually means postponing pleasure for a few years. Totally worth it.

~~~~~~

Third, while everyone needs a cell phone, not every needs the latest smartphone with a high monthly bill. Sacrifice a little now to have the life you want later. Track your expenses and get them under control now to build wealth you'll enjoy later. I've found that people are happier when they manage their money.

How to Stop Worrying About Money

I was not always wealthy. I grew up worrying if we'd be able to stay in our house another day. Then I moved in with my Dad and worried if an uninvited guest might break into our cheap apartment. Once I was out on my own, the worry increased, and at one point, I was ten dollars away from homeless. I was late on my rent, and my landlord said that if I didn't bring him at least $10 by 5:00, he would change the locks and have my stuff thrown out in the street.

I sold my suit for $10 that day and I've never been homeless. But that episode caused me to worry about money like never before, and all that worry caused other unproductive things to happen.

Thankfully, my mentor had a different perspective. He recognized that I had a scarcity mindset. I looked at the world like there was not enough to go around, so I was always angling to get my share. Angling caused stress, and it caused me to think more about getting a raise than about doing my job well.

He helped me realize that I'd always had enough. Even the $10 came through. And if it hadn't, I'd still have been okay. I had to admit that even if that landlord threw my stuff in the street, I had a place to go.

It was then I realized that the world really is a place of abundance. There does seem to be plenty of air, water, land, and food to go around. One look at Craigslist and we see thousands of jobs going unfilled, so there are plenty of jobs. Some of those jobs pay more in an hour than most people in the world make in a week. America really is a land of opportunities where people who study and work can build wealth far greater than anytime in history. No, it's not perfect, but neither is it a place of scarcity. The USA is a land of abundance.

~~~~~~

If you want to stop worrying about money, start believing in abundance.

~~~~~~

Stop listening to advertisers who try to make you feel inadequate by associating their stuff with a good life. The system they propose is based on outward appearances and material goods. Their premise is that the life you want begins with buying their thing. Let me ask you, has owning something new and shiny ever given you a *lasting* feeling of self worth, or has it just led to deeper feelings of inadequacy and the need for another shiny object?

While you're at it, stop listening to manipulative politicians (redundant phrase, I know). Listen to leaders, not the liars who manipulate people by creating a scarcity mindset, and trying to make you believe they will give you some free stuff. Remember that the government earns nothing by delivering value. Governments tax citizens to produce revenue. Nothing is free. Someone pays for it, and eventually, *you are the someone paying*. Don't believe fear mongers and manipulators.

~~~~~~

The good life starts on the inside.

~~~~~~

Believe that your paycheck provides you with all the things you *need* to be happy. Stop blaming others for your unhappiness--that hasn't worked since Cain tried it out on Abel. Your happiness is completely within your control. If you need more money to be happy, and you might if it's hard to afford rent and food, then relax and decide you will find the answers you need. Start reading. Hang out with people who have better money management skills than you do. Read books, listen to podcasts offering tips to do more with less. Soon enough, you'll have more.

Remind yourself that you can learn new skills more valuable than the skills you now possess, and those new skills will pay you more and give you more choices than ever. You can create new streams of income by learning more and investing your time well.

You want to stop worrying about money? Manage what money you *do* have. Cut expenses. As you reduce your worry, your creative mind will see more opportunities, and solve bigger problems. That side hustle you always dreamed of is within reach once your mind is right.

The next section can be a tough one. Money is tough to manage, but at least it doesn't talk back. Managing relationships, however, involves managing people and people do talk back. Despite the difficulty involved, if we do not manage our relationships, they'll go off the tracks and we will wish we had.

You're almost done. Chapter 10 is the last one in the series, and also the most rewarding!

That's a fact,
Jack

10

MANAGE RELATIONSHIPS OR WISH YOU HAD

Watch the chapter 10 video at https://vimeo.com/253136809

Like money management, few of us were taught how to manage our relationships so that drama decreases and happiness increases.

In this chapter, you will learn:

- How to manage relationships.
- How to choose which relationships to maintain.
- When to abandon a relationship.

How to Manage Relationships

I've often heard that "managing relationships" sounds like manipulating people to get something, but it's not that at all. When someone is manipulative, they're *mis*managing a relationship by deceiving people. Manipulation attempts to remove another person's freedom by deceiving them. Relationship management adds to their freedom by using honesty and care.

~~~~~~

To manage a relationship means doing your part to remain at peace with others, to give them more freedom to choose their own path, and to create an atmosphere where authentic love increases.

~~~~~~~~~~~~~~~~~~~~~~~~~~~~~~~~~~~~~~

In an earlier chapter, you created a list of things you do that cause you either to gain energy or that drain energy from you. Take another look at your gains and drains list. Are there any people on that list?

If you limited the list of gains and drains to tasks, that's not a problem. Simply repeat the exercise while thinking about all the people with whom you regularly interact.

Create a simple classification system. I've found that people fall into four categories: acquaintances, allies, friends, and toxic. Even family members fall into those four categories.

Acquaintances want to be with you but add little value to your life. Allies add value, you enjoy working with them, but they're not people you relax with socially. Friends are your true friends, the ones you hang out with, with whom you can be completely at ease, and the ones who are always for your success. Toxic people are those that give you a bad feeling whenever you're with them, they're the negative critics who tear you down and make you feel like you drank poison.

Relationship management is all about choices. Some choices are hard.

Choose Which Relationships to Maintain

Identifying the people who add to your energy means knowing who to spend more time with.

Spend the most time with people who add value to your life.

Acquaintances repeatedly ask you to lunch, but you always feel you'd rather not go. Often, you have to be around them because you work together or they're at every family gathering, and you just can't get away. Be nice to them, but limit contact. Often, these are people who have an agenda. They're not really interested in your thing, they're interested in their thing. They will distract you from your goals by trying to pull you into helping them achieve their goals.

Allies, on the other hand, want to win and they also want you to win. They see an alignment between their goals and yours. They add value by helping you achieve your goals while they achieve theirs. These people energize you. In your career and business relationships, health, wealth building, and spiritual life, allies are gold! Spend as much time as possible with allies.

Friends are people who know you and love you anyway.

Friends love you back. They add tremendous energy. You brighten up just thinking about seeing them. But, and this is a big-as-Kim-Kardashian-but, *you do not want to do business with friends.* Too many people make the mistake of doing business with their friends and family only to see those relationships deteriorate because doing business adds an unusual level of stress to relationships.

Let's say you start a restaurant and ask friends and family for help with the upfront costs. Your favorite uncle dips into his retirement and invests $50,000, and two people that you've been friends with since high school each invest another $50,000. You put in your money and sweat and things are going great, until they're not.

Perhaps, this was your first or second attempt at starting a business. Maybe, you did not follow the guidelines for creating a successful business. Maybe you did not have a proven coach to guide you through the traps of entrepreneurship. You tried to go cheap and lost it all--hey, I sure have, so no judgment here. Whatever the reason, imagine the business failed and everyone lost money.

Your friends and favorite uncle will probably forgive you for losing their money. As responsible investors, they knew the risk. I've had my share of losses and have learned plenty from each one. Shoot, my losses are the main reasons for my successes, but those losses were still painful!

The thing is, even if your uncle and your friends forgive you, you will have a terrible time forgiving yourself. You'll create new limiting beliefs that will torture those three relationships everytime you see those people. Your friends are worth more than financial success. Many people have ignored this reality and found it to be true as they lost friends to a failed business venture. It's too great a risk to go into business with friends.

Maintain relationships with allies and friends by investing time in them, knowing their needs, and helping where you can. Maintain relationships with acquaintances but don't invest as much as you do with your allies and friends. Avoiding acquaintances completely can be politically dangerous while spending too much time with them is distracting. That leaves one category to avoid at all cost.

When to Abandon a Relationship

People who suck the life out of you are those to avoid. I call them toxic because being around them feels like you've been poisoned.

The first time I realized I had toxic friends, I was 19. All my close friends were going nowhere fast--they were all toxic. One was dealing drugs. One was drinking at work. One had gotten his girlfriend pregnant and just left her to figure out what to do with the baby. One was kicked out by his parents. None of them were educating themselves, none were happy at work, none talked positively about their future prospects. I hated to do it, but I had to find new friends.

One of those guys died of a heart attack before he turned 30, one was shot by his girlfriend, another went to jail, another found his way and now owns a successful business, and one died bitter and broken by liver cancer. There were multiple divorces, terrible relationships with their kids and jobs they hated. It looks like I made the right choice, doesn't it?

Maybe you're like me and were raised to believe that family are in a special relationship category that has to be maintained no matter what. That is a nice sounding platitude meant to hold families together by creating loyalty. Unfortunately, it's manipulative, untruthful, and often used by predators to guilt people into staying around while they dump poison on their family members.

When you find yourself drinking poison, stop drinking poison! Yes, it takes courage. Be courageous.

You get to choose who you spend time with. There is never a good reason to spend time with someone who sucks the life out of you.

When you have a relationship with a toxic person, show them the boundary line clearly. I've found that explaining how I feel often works. Saying something like,

> *When you [belittle me, rant against my political ideology, criticize my work, poke fun at my weight, tell racist jokes, mock my religion, or you can insert whichever of their behaviors triggers your negative emotions], I feel [angry, fearful, sad, or disgusted] and that causes me to lose confidence. When you treat me that way, it takes me a day or two to overcome it.*

> *I love you and respect your opinion. I'm asking you to respect my beliefs and goals. If you cannot do that, then I cannot be around you.*

That'll get their attention. If they really love you and respect you, they'll apologize and behave. If not, they'll throw more poison on you. Either way, you'll have your answer on how much time to spend with them.

As you manage your relationships, you'll find yourself with a whole lot less of what you don't want, and whole lot more of what you do want. And that is my reason for writing this book.

That's a fact,
Jack

Watch the bonus chapter video at https://vimeo.com/253166588

Hey! You made it!

Congratulations! You have completed *Mindset for Success*. You now have the knowledge that highly successful people use to build the best possible life. You possess time-tested tactics to help you get what you want: robust health, increasing wealth, fulfilling relationships, empowering spiritual life, and a meaningful career.

Celebrate your accomplishment! Ice cream sounds good about now, doesn't it?

Let me know how you're doing and, by all means, send me your feedback on the program. I'm always looking for ways to get better.

At this stage, most people have two comments. First, they tell me they wish they'd found this information sooner. For that, I am profoundly grateful, and I invite you to share the book with your allies and friends. I'm even happy if you send it to the toxic people in your life--maybe they can get some help before they chase everyone away!

Second, people ask me "What's next, Jack?" Well, there's plenty. To learn more, please contact us at jackallenphd.com.

I'd be honored to speak to your civic group, team, or event. It is my pleasure to serve you. I wish you success and 100,000 blessings!

That's a fact,
Jack

Jack M. Allen, Ph.D.

ABOUT THE AUTHOR

Dr. Jack Allen is the Founder of Dynamic Coaching in Austin. He focuses on developing the mindset that leads to success in all areas of life. Not just financial success, but relationships, health, career, even spirituality. He has worked with over 750 clients from all walks of life.

Jack has built 11 successful organizations and learned from some epic failures. He knows the mindset, ethics, motivational tactics, neuroscience, and practical skills necessary to find successful, abundant living. His "no BS" approach gives fast, actionable results, not hazy woo-woo.

He is Adjunct Professor of Business Ethics at Concordia University Texas, and trains examiners for the Ethics in Business and Community Award. Jack's Ph.D. is in ethics and managerial psychology with emphases in cultural reconciliation and economics.

Jack has delighted over 100,000 people and annoyed at least that many with audiences in every major US city as well as Ireland, Kenya, Rwanda, and Guatemala. He's a funny, candid, thought-provocateur.

His money-back guarantee sets the industry standard for integrity.

Fun Facts
- Jack is happily married (still!) to his high school sweetheart.
- He has two grown children and a dog who really like him.
- He flunked out of college, got back in and made the Dean's List.
- He once visited the world's largest slum where he taught 2nd graders to read.
- He grew up orange-headed in Austin, Texas.

Credibility
- SME: organizational culture development, ethics, neuroscientific motivation
- Ph.D. in ethics and managerial psychology
- Board Certified Coach
- Over 1,500 keynotes to over 100,000 people
- Over 750 clients
- Delivery in every major US city and international settings
- Experience in corporations, academia, nonprofits, and churches
- 2010 Baldrige Award (with K&N Management)
- 2010 Ethics in Business and Community Award
- 2015 Individual Finalist, Ethics in Business and Community Award

Jack M. Allen, Ph.D.

BONUS READING

Mindset

- *How to Win Friends and Influence People*, by Dale Carnegie
- *Think and Grow Rich*, by Napoleon Hill
- *As a Man Thinketh*, by James Allen
- *Mindset: The New Psychology of Success*, by Carol Dweck, Ph.D.

Health

- *Margin: Restoring Emotional, Physical, Financial, and Time Reserves to Overloaded Lives*, by Richard Swenson, M.D.
- *Get Fit!: The Last Fitness Book You will Ever Need*, by Larry North

Wealth

- *The Greatest Salesman in the World*, by Og Mandino
- *Rich Dad Poor Dad: What the Rich Teach Their Kids About Money That the Poor and Middle Class Do Not!*, by Guy Kawasaki
- *The Total Money Makeover: A Proven Plan for Financial Fitness*, by Dave Ramsey
- *The Investor's Manifesto: Preparing for Prosperity, Armageddon, and Everything in Between*, by William J. Bernstein

Career

- *The First 90 Days: Proven Strategies for Getting Up to Speed Faster and Smarter*, by Michael D. Watkins
- *Influence: The Psychology of Persuasion*, by Robert B. Cialdini
- *It's Called Work for a Reason!: Your Success Is Your Own Damn Fault*, by Larry Winget

Relationships

- *Communication Miracles for Couples: Easy and Effective Tools to Create More Love and Less Conflict*, by Jonathan Robinson
- *The 5 Love Languages: The Secret to Love that Lasts*, by Gary Chapman
- *Dealing with People You Can't Stand: How to Bring Out the Best in People at Their Worst*, by Rick Kirschner and Rick Brinkman

Spirituality

- *The Ragamuffin Gospel: Good News for the Bedraggled, Beat-Up, and Burnt Out*, by Brennan Manning
- *The Spirit of the Disciplines: Understanding How God Changes Lives*, by Dallas Willard
- *God Is Not One: The Eight Rival Religions That Run the World*, by Stephen Prothero

Made in the USA
Middletown, DE
19 January 2019